# A-DRIFT

*poems by*

# Amy-Sarah Marshall

*Finishing Line Press*
Georgetown, Kentucky

*drift*
: the slow movement of something carried by wind or water
   : a pile of something that has been blown by the wind
      : a course something appears to be taking
         : the meaning of something said or implied


*adrift*
: without motive power and without anchor or mooring
   : without ties, guidance, or security
      : free from restraint or support

# A-DRIFT

*TO MY FAMILY*
*For Phin, who taught me to swim.*
*For Sam, who goes with the flow.*
*For Lisa, my lifeguard and love.*

Copyright © 2022 by Amy-Sarah Marshall
ISBN 978-1-64662-954-1 First Edition
All rights reserved under International and Pan-American Copyright Conventions. No part of this book may be reproduced in any manner whatsoever without written permission from the publisher, except in the case of brief quotations embodied in critical articles and reviews.

## ACKNOWLEDGMENTS

"Shelled" first appeared in *The Dewdrop*
"On Your Radar" first appeared in the *Lavender Review*

Publisher: Leah Huete de Maines
Editor: Christen Kincaid
Cover Art: Amy-Sarah Marshall
Author Photo: Lisa Green
Cover Design: Elizabeth Maines McCleavy

Order online: www.finishinglinepress.com
also available on amazon.com

Author inquiries and mail orders:
Finishing Line Press
PO Box 1626
Georgetown, Kentucky 40324
USA

# Table of Contents

Adrift ............................................................................. 1

First ............................................................................... 2

Evidence ....................................................................... 3

Shelled .......................................................................... 4

By the Sea .................................................................... 5

One Wing ..................................................................... 7

Walking on Water ....................................................... 8

Miracle of the Fishes ................................................ 10

Growing Soft ............................................................. 11

Caving ........................................................................ 12

Mercy .......................................................................... 15

Catch & Release ........................................................ 22

Failure ........................................................................ 23

On Your Radar .......................................................... 24

Between Two ............................................................. 25

Memory ...................................................................... 26

Many Waters ............................................................. 27

Mermaids & Pirates .................................................. 32

Forecast ...................................................................... 33

Aphrodite ................................................................... 34

The Hunger Moon .................................................... 35

## ADRIFT

Of course, I was born in the ocean, at sea, over
And over again. I never knew placidity, surface
Tension. I rolled with the gulps,
Called to the gulls, surged in the red
Strides of the swells that stalked
The continental edge. I knew better than
To swim, to force my body
Through. I survived lightly,
Holding only air, wanting
Only what held, spilled
Me. This swollen origin
Above beneath beyond
Shaped and sized me
Rocked and shocked me
Into a self that never
Needed anchor or buoy, boat
Or plasticine float. Only now,
Landed, am I adrift
With longing, aching
Like a plough that grinds
At the ground, gristle
Of meat, dirt and rock, the thick
Resistant clay, and mud, repeating
Its solidarity. I miss
The easy split of
Froth, the drift
Of currents, the stars
On watch. To be swallowed
Whole in the darkness. To cry
And piss and bleed in the intimacy
Of knowing what I am, inside
And out. Of course,
I am lost. Where is
The life preserver for one
Standing in the static
Of the arid, rooted world,
Still but seething,
Breathing but drowning?

## FIRST

Into the park, and words start running
from me—ice loosens into

water. The geese wash their wings
in the mint-green rush; a stretch of sand

pock-marked with the memory of their morning
feet. January arches over, a single branch

crusted with
what's left of last year, bunched

scallops of fungi, layered
and sticky as meringue, hard

as bone. Roots confuse the
scene. Winter in the picture

books: a flat lap of snow.
Here, the page opens to a slick,

crimson sky. Vines dress the grey
stiffness in rich peach. Birches,

maples, ash in backbends of relinquishment
to the present. The past flakes

away. Something harder than a diamond
rips through my throat;

something sweeter than tears
rushes down. The myriad things dividing

life from life and rinsing
the wind. What else

can I wish for? What else
can I say? Strike the balance

of a pose and hold it. When the
Wind comes, sway.

**EVIDENCE**

She sits in the church
parking lot shoving
an entire white
cake in her mouth.

She opens the card I sent, the one
with the Black
mother. She knows I am trying
to disown her.

She would often compare
our skin tones, call me
pink vs. her yellow, talk about
how dark she could
get in the sun, enough
for her dad to mistake her
for "a Mexican." She would point
out my freckles, evidence
sure as footprints that
my father had been there
in my genetic code, making
a mess. Her nose, she
said, was too blunt, while mine
was a ski jump; her
forehead square, mine perfectly
curved. She oiled
herself up and laid flat
as dough on the concrete
stoop, baking and browning,
no discernable burn. I watched her
darken, pool. I shoved whole
hours in my mouth. I waited,
a pale valence, on the inside
of the sliding glass door.

**SHELLED**

in the litter of stones that glitter
the damp sand

of a winter day sucking
on a warm, green river

you touch an open clamshell
each twin pocket

slim and pale
as a fingernail

but cocked like a locket
from a mother's drawer

without a photo to describe
what she held

dear just escape or shiny
relinquishment

and your own lonely
brain picking through

**BY THE SEA**

In the park
By the beach. Pacific
Gloating and fat
Thrashing wet.
A rhythm of greed,
She pinned you to the tree and
Kissed you. Kissed you good,
Breathing ocean
On your breath. Salt or grit
Stuck in your teeth.

To the roar of the water,
In the heat of a first summer,
The Colonia girls, their
Murmurs a
Blurring in the dusk.

They watched. Moved closer.
Two-by-fours
To bash her gold-flecked
Glasses; splintered
Paper money fleeing
A piñata, falling
Sparks of color over her legs.

No screams. Only one
Nasty word you'd never heard of spit
From a candied tongue.

Till the grass sighs
In your arms
The hard-smacked
Drum of your back
Look at it, all of it, happening, easy,
As easy
As the sun, relaxing
Its back
On the pale
World.

So easy (no screams)
Kiss another girl kiss
To the beat (no candy)
Of those sticks
Of that water

**ONE WING**

Geese dunk their wings
    in the water    In the blue-green light of the
River    Eyes touch the limber

Yogi trees    luminous

softness    Delirium of midday

Patterns  currents
Forming    shattering    All mind-object    objects of
the mind

Turtles blink
a dozen suns    Indra's sleepy eyes
swallow the world

Multifoliate and inviolate
Myriad and zero
Nest and neutron star

World without end and world

Within    One
wing in
    the winter river
               shivering

## WALKING ON WATER

But why would you want to walk on
Water, is what I keep asking.
Why not dip and dunk
In, why all these crowds overcome with
Bliss for a miracle with no point to it?
What's wrong, I ask you, with *swimming*?

And it's not just watersports: There's all this
Wanting to fly *over rainbows or away* or *like a bird* or
With airplanes, lyrics that echo wings
On women from 300 BC
Carved in the ruins, from India
To Chaldea, dreams of jetpacks (who
Doesn't dream of a jetpack?)

Take the plunge, I say, the float,
The holding of breath, the yacht
Or boat, the rowing or tipping under, the knowing
You're caught in an element that won't forgive you
For breathing, go in—
I mean, the fancy footwork, all well
And good—the flashy camp when you're a deity
On a promotional tour trying to break into the big time—

A better miracle I can believe: the time
We were swimming and saw three gleaming fins, how
We screamed for the shore—*Jaws* theme thumping—only to
Turn back, watch three bottlenoses brim
In a glittering lick of salt and laughing
At our mistake, our lack of faith—
       I mean, we've all been
There, out of our depths, in danger, only to look
Back later and see we had the company of
Something rather sweet—

To the men in white robes strutting like Superman,
To the vamping angels, I say: Sink,
Sink below the surface
Get gracious with gravity, go
Under, jump on the mattress, run down this hill, get

Grounded with me. Maybe then
I'll be impressed, then I'll see you
As magnificent, the way you
Have a body and use it
To be a body in this world—

## MIRACLE OF THE FISHES

As August lolls its long, flat tongue—
and it's a hot one—fat and damp, my heart
climbs down to the water
like the white-hot moon
when it needs to cool
off; I am so very sad and raw
and tender to the touch;
I have so little and need so
much and there is no reassurance, no body
of water that can hold me enough—

Which is not to say there are no miracles.
As I stretch out in the soft
lap of the lake's edge
a multitude of little silver fishes
Feed from my skin, nip at existence,
swallow my insistence on
being here. Each delicate bite,
and the infinite bliss of the summer
burns into a simmer. My resistance grows
a little slimmer and I give in
a little more to what I
cannot control. Which is
the ten thousand sorrows that
thrive, divide, and multiply into
these tiny flashing slivers
who swim in the water
and eagerly feed
on the ten thousand joys of the sun.

## GROWING SOFT

This is one of those evenings when the air's cool and dry
like the soft cheek of a grandmother who smells
like lotion and lip balm and roses and plastic baggies full of gumdrops
or maybe she is slightly rotting, giving off the scent
of disintegration, the nibbling of bacteria and mold, a tree
fallen in the woods being taken down into the dark
earth—urine maybe; fresh bread; stale teeth; crusted spit—

but anyway, she is soft. Just like the trees tonight, lofty
and gentle in the moody blush before twilight, the purpling
buoyancy arching over with a tenderness one would like
to believe in, like romanticism, the kind of nature Keats
could stick his cleats in—

—the kind of night I'd want to be with you, on a deck,
in a hammock, dipped a bit in the sweat of the day but
relishing the delicate chill against the back of our necks—
whatever wrecking we'd been through, this emollient
rocking cradle of a sky would make us feel cherished—
certainly I'd be cherishing you—

nothing important has to happen
on a night like this. Just breathing
is fantastic. Just being with you
is bliss. Your imagined lips would make Keats grip
the edge of the line like a grandmother grabs
your cheek and spits your chin to make
it shine—oh she is definitely bending down
to brush the hair out of your eyes—and her limbs
sway, and the lilac bursts out singing, and the nightingale's
song is brimming, and I can almost believe
you are here now, swimming with me
in this lisp of the soft darkness—

# CAVING
*To Julia*

1.
In the packed mud sludge of night—
that time that buries the bodies and bones
of dreams, where nothing seems
like it could move against the
sucking, succulent dark—
the voice. That voice. Screaming
along the naked tracks like a train
but it is not a train, and
it is not stopping. It is a living
thing, picking its way
across each spike of
your spine, each shrieking
refrain pricks another
line of nerves like
tight guitar twine.
Possum, skunk, fox? What
undesirable, homeless
child of the razed trees
has found in grief
the ability to crack
open the moon? Oh the ache
of the plaintive note breaking
into your house, thieving you of
the security you've kept so
closely locked up, smooth
and clean as an egg. Something
caves in you as you listen
with a dry throat of your own,
something so long boarded
up against the weather.
The worst kind of haunting.

2.
And then there's waking to
the other side of the gold
morning, the small white dogs wiggling
through the rough patch
of another rushed week
to this other side where
a grateful steam of tea licks your cheek
like it likes you, and you take it,
and the lack of resistance
becomes a drop of relief, like
honey when you need it in
a stiff drink; like a drink, when you
need it more than honey, like
the cursing you can sometimes
keep from coursing up the roots
of you, basement to bedroom, feeding
the untended desires
you have folded nicely
and put away with
the lacy doilies
that dolloped a grandmother's
dresser, dripping with the conceit
that furniture could take
the place of eternity, lasting
and valuable, unlike
the flesh that binds you and keeps
you, at least until it sheds
you and flees you—recedes deeply into
the packed mud of
your last night.

3.
What else do we ask but
*what lasts?* You grab the monkey
bars and grasp that you can't
hang on forever, but you still
tether your heart to iron, sink
the weight of your love deep in
the ocean floor. You accept what
you get and try not to want more. You
deflect attention and neglect
the motion sickness that rises when
people leave, by various means, some
permanent. You never knew what
was meant by *firmament*, but it sounded
stronger than the sky, and you know,
you still feel nourished by the definition
you imagined, fed by the feeling that
somewhere, a footer of heaven dug
and filled so solid it will pass inspection
will hold up all the suffering and hope.
The swing on your tree moves
sometimes due to children, sometimes
due to wind, and sometimes, you sit
there and hang on with all your might, for
the rush of air that is almost flight to
feel your body move into the blue
almost but not quite beyond
your definition of *alive*.

## MERCY

It happens on a school day.
A school night.
Right after school.
On a bridge, near the concert hall.
In the gas station parking lot.
Near the train tracks.

In her bedroom.
In her father's bed. Out back.
At her best friend's house.
In her bed.
On her pillow.
Against her neck.
It happens under the bleachers or
In a field or
After the party and the dark night
Swirling around the Merryville the
Steubenville the Oakland the Charlottesville
Landscape is cold enough that she can
Feel the warning of winter in
Her bones coming up in bumps
Along the edges of her arms, the territory
Of her skin, her territory,
Her body losing warmth.
She doesn't have a coat.
She is in jeans.
A nightgown.
A prom dress.
Kneesocks.
Keds.
With a cell phone.
No keys.
Keys.
Her blonde hair her black
Hair her very thin strands of pale
Hair that soak in her mouth when
She's sleeping, her thick ponytail,
Her knotted curls.
That morning, she kissed her mother on the
Cheek reluctantly, didn't want to
Get too mushy or mess up her

Lip gloss. That afternoon she had plans
To go shopping. She was out on a
Date. She was hoping to get
Laid. She was ready for
High school. She was scared of
The lightning outside and was looking
For comfort, she was desperate for
Affection because she was five and
No one paid attention, she has a big
Family, she is a foster child, her father
Is a mayor, she was adopted and no
One ever lets her forget it. She is
Beloved. Someone must
Love her. We want to
Believe. We pray for mercy
As if god and the angels are holding out on
Us, they have the coordinates of
Her location, they know the right
Button to push to make
Miracles happen, get snappy with
It, we don't care to learn any
Lessons, for window options to
This particular kind of closed,
Battened-down door.

Please. Open.
She is innocent.
We are innocent.
When she was born she was without
Sin and we beg for you to
Give in and let them find her.
When they find her,
When they find her body,
When they find out,
When there is no
Trace and the news gets tired or
The journalists stay rabid or
The phone rings every day or
Never with tips with bad tips
With the right tips when
The stranger sees her face in

The window behind the white
Linen burka when the hikers
Take a moment to remember what
She looks like there on the mountain
And they call, when a neighbor makes
The call, when a dog smells
Something.
When the search is never
Over.

When the story gets
Questioned.
When the memories come up like
Weeds into her storyline and she tries
To yank them out by their
Roots and they only keep
Growing and choking.
When arrests are made.
When charges are dropped.
When charges are dropped and she is
Dropped from the cheerleading squad when
She cannot move on when she moves
On when she cannot move
Any longer when she does not
Move when the whole country is
Moved when no one is moved to do
Anything because she is really
A he and who knows he probably just
Ran away don't they do that
Kind of thing.

When people think
She asked for it.
When people have no idea
What he does to her
What he did to her
What he will do to her
When they look
Past and through and away.
When they think they care
But they are just

High on scandal and fascinated
By other people's
Suffering.
Who among us is not
Suffering. Suffer the little
Children. And a little bit
Addicted.

The lord is the great I Am and he is
With her, I say, I say to myself,
Or has he abandoned her,
How can god let it happen and happen
And happen
Again. It's an old question. But
She is just eleven. She is just sixteen.
Twenty. Five.
She is my friend's niece, she is my
Best friend, she is someone I should have
Met, a girl on the TV screen, she is
My mother, a headline in the paper, she is
Their daughter. She is our
Child, our sister, ours.
God is the great I am but
What are we, the little I ams the
Little lambs the lost
Sheep the wolves dressed up
For hunting season which is
All the time, which one are you?

Both? Little Red Riding Hood
Sneaks into the woods and she
Loves flowers, and what happened to
My grandfather that dad that
Couple that loser that man that
Football player and his friends those
Kids, what happens when
They see her, what is it in them that
They are predators, boys will be
Boys, I don't believe it, I don't
Believe that my son is bred to
Destroy that my daughter is

Deserving of this because she is
Not a boy. My daughter.
I watch their faces, I hear their
Names even when I don't want to,
Alexis, Sage, Morgan, Elizabeth,
Helen, Katy, Mary. My daughter,
The deep grief, the fierce fear,
The waiting, the crazed seething,
The rage, the nightmares, the lack
Of relief, or undoing. Learning to tie
A knot. Or not.
Pacing.
A race in place.
The traced steps, the retraced steps
The belief that steps can be taken,
Measures, we can measure this,
He measures our days, the birds
In the field.
We can find a way.
We can find her.
We can find her.
Hope and desperation.
When the phone
Doesn't ring, when she doesn't
Come home, when she comes home
Bleeding, when she never
Comes. My ears are
Ringing. Where are you, I am
Screaming, to her, into the void
Of unknowing where god is
Supposed to be, clouded,
As silent as a forest is silent,
Going on about its business of birds
And snakes and skunks and deer feeding
On the groundcover, each other and not speaking
About where my girl is, where her
Body is hiding. All those movies
With the magical mice rescuing the
Girl, but in real life, they are harmless
And I am helpless and the needles
Prick and the curses stick and the enemy

Is the one who shows up on his
Horse in his van at the bedside table
On the side of the road. He goes for her
Heart. He seals the deal. He makes his
Mark. He steals the base. He does his
Duty. He makes a stab in the dark. He
Forces the issue. He nails the case. He
Takes the cake. He dominates
The field. He stakes his ground. He pounds
Out the win.
He gets the girl.

I sit in my car, waiting, radio off, rain
Slicing air, I am weeping for
My own daughter
Whose sweetness is so singular, so
Very much her, how can
I keep her, empower her or tower
Her, my bones ache, their stories,
Their real-life bodies breaking
Under the weight of what
Happens to them,
To the girls, to us,
What happens to our girls. Lolita squishes
Her eyes at the bright sky, next week, 11
Months, next month, a whole year, he's
Been gone. She counts.
They all count.
Each parent counts their children's days,
The hours they sleep, the weeks till
They arrive, the days they go not wetting
The bed, the years they turn more years
And leave, the constant counting of
Their lives, as if time will amount to
Something permanent if we just
Keep track, as if knowing the number
Of their days will keep them safe,
And at some point, won't it be too
Long for her to be gone?
Elizabeth looks up, into the sunlight
And eventually nods when

They call her name. A farmer trips
On Morgan's femur. Helen escapes
In her mind only. A zip line flight.
Katy makes it back to her hotel
Room. Mary learns to say no and kick
And fight. Or we don't know and we go
Through the motions, we keep
On moving through our days
In the deliberate shrugging away of
What else am I going to do,
All of this wretchedness and the maddening
Circling in the sky that is
Always coiling closer
To the decay at the center, where we wait
Under veils and hats and the swaying
Flags and posterboard displays, help
Wanted, wanted signs, the unwanted
Camera, the oh-so desired media presence.
It is all darkness.
And madness. The dissolution
Of all things, except the rash panic
That something could have been done.
With our awful hunger pangs of love
Please God, feed us in this hour of need with
The precious gift
Of understanding that will
Make something of this grief, of this,
Her disappearance, her
Abduction, her death, her rape,
Her precious life
Every minute of it
And make it okay
That nothing ever is or will be.
Have mercy, someone,
Anyone, you. Because she's
Crossing the bridge. Laying her
Head down to sleep.
She's crossing her legs.
She's leaving the store.
It's happening.

## CATCH & RELEASE

Hard to explain why
and how, in the quiet, as
everything rises to the surface
my one small consolation is
the certain rock against
the window, and possibly a shattering

through the glass quickly and
darkly, one last pattern in
the smash. Reality will breathe
through, and that will be that.

The snow hasn't left
the fractured mountains.
Every effort, every clinging, the earth
ringing with the sting of pipes
and drills and instruments of craving
for more and more, the surfaces surging
feverishly back and heaving whole
populations up and over. You know
it, don't you, how blessed you
are to have the nerves available
for reading this very sentence, this
instance of English arranged for you
just you at this very moment,
to have and to hold till you choose
to let it go? Catch and release, the story
goes; we wait and wait for the hidden
fish to take the bait. We gloat
with the pulled prize, toss
it in and start once more to wait.

We call this benevolence. The fish will rise
again but whatever returns,
whatever endures, well, that's all
good and well but what matters is that
you are with me now, in these words, these rocks
I am heaving in your direction, tossing
into the water, at your window,
with my little hope.

# FAILURE
*for phin*

I stood at the door to our house
your infant brother in my arms
left you sitting with
your father on the brown couch.
Your eyes buttoned up against
the cold: opaque, shiny.
I explained to my choking car that
you were old enough and
it was good for you, that
it was fair and we were bucking up.
None of those things were
true. I nursed the baby each night
you were gone, tears pooling
on his closed, oblivious eyes.
And you, what did you do
with those evenings? Wrap
them up in the green baby blanket
that has since gone missing or bury
each hour in the jewelry box you never used?
Where did you keep the kisses I blew
from the cracking doorstep,
so they wouldn't chill your
sleepy cheeks or weigh upon
your heavy mind? And all the dark wind of
that winter coming in through the
open door, the way it stayed
and held you by the throat so
that you never cried, or spoke,
or tried to follow? And how, my love,
will I ever repent enough to open
what closed between us?

## ON YOUR RADAR

The sobbing outside the window, you ran to it,
jumped out of bed in the middle of the night
and scowled at the stars. Suffering
attracts you, disaster a magnet. You
constantly scan the atmosphere
for fate's pulling of the carpet, for what's
coming next to rob your
already sparsely furnished storehouse
of peace and precious things.

And meanwhile, love, I am waiting for you to
notice me. I rise every morning, tenderly, turning
toward you with a whole bright heart. As you stand
at the window, searching the dark for the source
of the pain you are bracing to take, I wait
for you, a veil of tears on my face. How carefully
you turn and twist the knobs, decipher
static with your tender, generous ear. The voice
you need to hear is calling from your own dark window.

**BETWEEN TWO**

Some people seem like God,
In his Hoover aspect, sent them to
Remind me of my imperfections, file
Away my darling little sins—she
Was like that, all dark and doubting
Eyes that took everything in, let none of it
Out. Every word I said was a lie, even
When it wasn't, or a shabby, second-hand
Coat, smelling of wet armpits and cheese.

One day we tried to distinguish between
*Trusting* and *liking*, and couldn't do it. We
Roped our toes and fingers through
The holes of her backyard hammock,
The nearby channel water tasting
The light of stars in hungry gulps. Her hair
Was like the water, long and heavy and reflecting.
She could sit like that, brooding, or putter
Around the house, picking up a book
Or a feather, whatever. When she
Clasped my hand, I knew what household
Objects felt like, close and chosen.

I was wrong, of course. She wasn't a spy.
She was kind, watching and listening. Then
I lost her. I was the one who didn't pay
Attention. I was the one, when we swam
In the channel, slipping and clinging.
Her hair spread in the water like a spill, and both
Were dark and waving. I floated
In them both. And I couldn't distinguish
Between the two.

**MEMORY**

Do you even remember loving me? Does that dark night cry at the window,
pawing at you to let her in? That one
where we decided to try, and the shadows
of the door soon darkened the pavement. We couldn't get enough of each
other. You wound yourself around me, that night. We came
to, out of the daze of daily life, into the warmth
of a world that started to exist, to lick at our knees like a sorry, lost dog.

When exactly did you kick it out into the cold? When did
you tire of wanting me? I can't remember, exactly; I can just tell, from
the way you stare at your phone and touch the screen of the
computer, that I am the last thing on
your mind, and you don't have the energy to
get up, let that dark night in, and feed it to make it stop whining.

## MANY WATERS

1.
        Still, over these many waters, it starts sinking in that
this is all there is
now
                and maybe all there ever was
then
        This
waiting, but for what. For what held us before,
for what we hope will erupt from the untouchable horizon
and give us a solid
                form
        a grip a rock a place to make the waves
stop.
        I hope we are between a rock and a hard place,
here, instead of between more of the same.    Is this water
           worthless?
      Can I throw my pennies in
and make a wish
        Will the tin and silver spin
              with the fish and deliver? Will I cast
my nets and drag back all the other
      drowned by sorrow and wishful
thinking?
        Something always happens
            if you are paying attention,
                a storm or a pelican pink
in the light of the dunking sun, could be
        the itch of salt in your throat
            smoothed by the silky tongue
of an oyster going down.
        What if this is all there is?
        How we lust for
           fields and forests and stretches of ice
to forage and stretch our legs.
        I long for a tree, the scabby bark
bruising my thighs as I tug my body
to the top
           the certainty
of dry
land
        maps and bricks

and making things stay
             with glue and tape.
                  I am afraid of this constant
                        unknowing state, the deliberate
laughing whack of the waves
                        that obscure any sign of
         arriving.

             By the way, am I the only one bothered
by this lack of information about
                  why we are here? From the looks of
it, most of you couldn't care
                        less.
             Meanwhile
                  days suck
at me, teething
                  on my soggy
sweaty skin, and every night
                  I'm dry eyed and in the dim mid of it
all the questions in my brain wreck
                        against the misery.

             We start out so happy and grateful
to be one of the lucky ones who
                  makes it here alive.
             And then we feel trapped and wonder
what's the point
                  of surviving
                  happenstance
                  circumstance
                  underpants
                        what does it all matter?
             The goddess stirs
her golden finger
                  in the water, we don't curry favor with her
by being good or nice or making all the right
                        choices and connections.
             It's not whatever floats your boat
but that the boat floats you
                  and what can you do but
be grateful for it, even

though
                    there's no one to thank
                    no one to blame
no one to pray to, not to be
saved from this.
        This is you
being saved.
        This is you
                safe.
        This is
what you asked for,
                    and this is what fate gave.
        Suck it up, sister.
                Isn't that what we say
to the animals?

        It is possible
we will become
                our own
island
        transportation
            will carry
the meaning of something
                that happens on the inside, when
the scenery knives you with its sharp
                    beauty, shaving the dull mud from
your eyes till you're no longer
                blind to the wonder of blue and gold rising
from the crisp, clashing waters.

2.
The compass is no prediction,
only a suggestion. It could be
the middle of the story,
or nearing the end, and I'll never know
if how I choose to stew
stretches or shrinks
what's left. If I can ditch
all my tools and plans
I might feel a little lighter,
a little fleeter, and the mist

on the morning's merge
of water and sky into light
will taste sweeter
as I breathe it all the way in,
as I take a bite of this day
like it matters to
be here, participating,
not just a witness on the sidelines
debating and baiting
bitterness.

(did I mention? I hate boats.
their terminology. the special
vocabulary for ordinary things, like
*right* and *left*.)

(that's a lie: I love boats, but they lie
on top of a surface that so easily slips
lost things in its deep pockets.)

The whales that wait for you
are beautiful and talk
about a great
hiding place. But
to god they remain
see-through, and to us
they are dark
and living caves, so it's really not
a recommended activity, testing the
waters of their patience.

P.S.
When I'm gone, someone else
will be rowing the lifeboats around
for exercise, pretending.

3.          Sink in
the question:
          Are tears lost in this mass
or do they merge

                        into something even larger
                                sweet
                                terrifying
the universe up there sparkling
                        with the dead stars still serving up
the light and cranking constellations
                        to tell us that we've drifted, to show us
time taking
                        shape, no other way to
measure
                        where we are.

        Not *where*, there is no where
but how
        only how.

        With no distinction between
                        the sky and the water,
between the planets
                        and the eyes of the wary, restless
fish we keep
                                I fear
                                every
                                plunge

        As the sun streaks
naked into the dark
                field of stars, the many waters
                        of the many cries, the many
                deep songs
                        one can hum along and feel
the inner surge of wordlessness cresting
                                pulling you into
the flow.
        We have nowhere else to go and
we are still moving,
                        aren't we?

## MERMAIDS & PIRATES

Pirates and mermaids, tigers and bats, the coast
blasts wave upon wave of fantastical myths regurgitated
from the Jungian crap-shoot depths. The treasure
chests of crab legs. The cravings. The untidy
buffet laps round the waiting boats of beef, the alligator shows luring
the hungry to come and feed on the idea of being dead
meat. The women and men stretched
in the sand, foaming at the teeth of the ocean, waiting
for some kind of mystical evaporation.

The seal mothers, we're told, get forced to choose between the searing
sun and their newborn young, who can't yet flipflop their way to
the protective wrap of the water; the sun drives the
mothers to the frenzy of self-preservation; their babies, left
behind, struggle against the sharp bite of the heat, of the waiting
wolf. All these choices we make. We think we're going
to save ourselves, and instead we're exposing the tender skins—
and that is vacation. The sacrificial lambs, the children broiling
on the beach; the helpless limbs of the parents, at the mercy
of the moon. Exhaustion. Who isn't a child here, calling out to
the forces beyond the horizon for a grace
that would match the strength of the taming source
of our civilization? Those tigers, sweating
in their original skins, those women strapped
into mermaid fins, swimming into the arms
of fry cooks in eye patches, making an extra
buck or two while the sweaty audience gnaws
on a lobster leg, clapping with greasy hands for
another day down the hatchet as another sun
bites down on what's left of the dusk.

**FORECAST**

various mists and clearings this morning    at some point
you won't be able to see
what's coming. what's not coming    at times
all the shapes and colors    will be revealed to you
like glory    you will swear the trees
have wings, singing    as they point their
green fingers    to the stars

and you will try to recall    the constellations when
the sky descends you will want to
keep going    so much at stake   so little time
not slowing down for weather    still

you could close your
eyes and notice    how gently
you are webbed    and blinded, so much closer
to knowing    the landscape thickness
when you drift and shift along with it
not driving    steering, gunning your hard and fast wishes

they say the visibility    is zero
you can't see and get around    the clouds
descending from the sky
don't even try it    give in to what exists

forgiveness    to the world, for being inconvenient
to yourself, for wanting to rush past what is
in fact   the weather    the glory
your one and only
try

## APHRODITE

*You look like the goddess who
comes out of the sea* she said
and I was, indeed, soggy
and drippy with remorse because
despite the force of the waves
smashed to sweetness against my
rigid form, I had a hard
time loosening up, letting
my sea-heavy hair come down
laughing when flattened on sand.

Flattery will get you.

Hanging out in my half-shell,
under the spell of my vexed
love-hate relationship with
the rough punches, the dunked pearls
the drunken gestures of my
origin, the sea, I can't
dismiss the glamorous hiss
of my own disabled myths.
Sometimes I get like this, hold
my wild girl in the ocean
with a fierce fist, put a hold
on her against the pull, I
hold still, immovable as
she kicks in the thrill and tilt
of the slosh and swirl and froth—
I stand like a skeleton coral,
long for the splash that could take
all of me under so I
could come up again, come up
truly, rising from
the dark and many waters
fumbling upward to the call
from my daughter's fearless lips
answering, unafraid, to
my true and everlasting
name.

## THE HUNGER MOON

Branches soak in the flood
Of an unglued winter river.
The crook of your arm
Can be a nutcracker
Or a pillow. We fish
And fish. The leaves
Reeled in mock
Our sanity, form the meals
Of the migrating force
Within us, forced down into
Solitude to
Sleep for months and months.

Sun just a little longer, just
One more shake of the pole,
Just one more hope that something substantial
Will come into our lives and multiply,
Perform the miracle of giving us
One more hope.

Your face begins to cloud, and breaking through
Could be the beginning or the end.

**Amy-Sarah Marshall** writes poetry, plays, children's stories, and fiction in Charlottesville, VA. She graduated with an MFA in Poetry from George Mason University and has published poems in the *Wisconsin Review, So to Speak, Streetlight, The Dewdrop, Phoebe, Brooklyn Review, Diner*, and other journals. In her day job, Amy-Sarah has worked as a web writer, editor, and content strategist, creating award-winning infographics and blog stories. A passionate activist, Amy-Sarah served on the Charlottesville Human Rights Commission and as founding president of the Charlottesville Pride Community Network, an LGBTQ+ community nonprofit. Currently, Amy-Sarah directs SafeCville, providing safe-space trainings to businesses, nonprofits, schools, and medical establishments throughout the area. A Los Angeles native, Amy-Sarah grew up in a religious theater missionary group and now practices mindfulness and Buddhism. She lives with her wife, 2 children, 2 dogs, and 2 cats.

CPSIA information can be obtained
at www.ICGtesting.com
Printed in the USA
BVHW040118140922
646955BV00003B/129